808.8

Middlebrook.

Life's seasons pass quickly.

DATE DUE

| JUN 12 '88 |
| AG 25 '91 |
| SE 8 '91 |

| 808.8 | 3658 |
| CLASS | ACC |

Middlebrook.
(LAST NAME OF AUTHOR)

Life's seasons pass quickly.
(BOOK TITLE)

DATE DUE	ISSUED TO
JUN 12 '88	
AG 25 '91	
SE 8 '91	

First Baptist Church Library
Tomball, Texas

Life's Seasons Pass Quickly

(A Collection of Columns
written for the *Tomball Sun*)

by: Charlie Middlebrook

Illustrations by: Evelyn Bouley

3658
Clear Fork Publishing
P.O. Box 569
Tomball, Texas   77375

Contents

Phone Call To A Friend 1
The Opera House 4
A Time To Remember 8
Sentimental Journey 11
Tender Memories 14
Places Of The Heart 17
The Red River Cemetery 20
Books 24
Leaving Home 27
Watching and Waiting 31
Fall 34
The Old House 37
Mixed Emotions 39
West Texas Football 42
The Quiet Fan 45
A Texas Patriot 49
Barefoot In The Snow 53
I Love You Mollie, But . . . 56
Life's Seasons Pass Quickly 60

Copyright © 1985
Charlie Middlebrook
Tomball, TX

Illustrations Copyright © 1985
Evelyn Bouley
Tomball, TX

Typography & Printing by
D. Armstrong Co., Inc.
Houston, Texas

Phone Call To A Friend

Ernest Morton Sprayberry is a banker in West Texas and a long time friend of my family. When the postal service failed to get a deposit up to his bank before some checks I wrote, Ernest Morton's computer wrote, suggesting that I might want to call my old friend pretty quickly.

It impressed me that the bank in my hometown had a computer that kept a check on those things and sent letters when needed, written in the same politely threatening style used by the machines that run Exxon and IBM. But it distressed me a little to think of good old Ernest Morton sitting down to a computer, sophisticated and tied into banks in Los Angeles and New York. There are some things you don't want to change. At the top of my list is the simplicity and innocence of the country people up home.

It worried me when I was ready to call him that he'd be different than I remembered, that he'd be formal and sound just like a banker in Houston. I wondered if I ought to call him Mr. Sprayberry. But I decided neither of us could have changed that much and that I'd call him Ernest, like always.

"Hello, Ernest? Charlie Middlebrook. How ya doin'?"

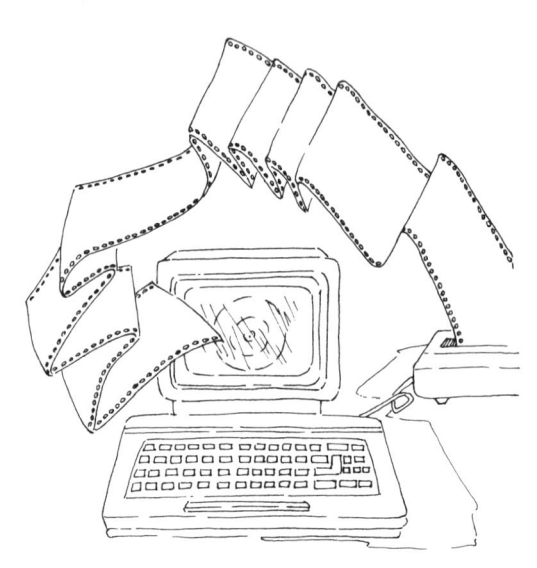

He said, "Well, I'm able to be up and takin' a little light nourishment." That meant he was doing fine.

"I got a letter from your computer about being overdrawn and it told me to call you real quick."

He said, "Hoo boy, sorry 'bout that. That thang's 'bout to drive me crazy. Man, I thank we mus' be tied inta ever big city in the world. You ever try dealin' with a banker in Chicago?"

"Well, I guess some of those checks were a bit warm. Do I need to pay ya for 'em?"

He said, "Shoot no! That computer don't run thangs around here as much as it thanks it does. I'll jus' push a couple of buttons and it'll forget it ever wrote ya. Hey, when ya comin' dove huntin'?"

"Soon, Ernest. Real soon. I need to put my feet under the same table with yours for a spell."

The Opera House

Few who read this will have heard of the Opera House in Anson, Texas. Those who have may be interested to know that it's going to be sold soon at a public auction.

Anson is in West Texas and has a wonderful square in the middle of town. The square is dominated by a beautiful old four-story courthouse that is topped by a capitol-like dome and has a great four-sided clock that can be seen from all over town.

The north-south highway divides and circles the courthouse, separating it from the buildings that face if from all sides. Outside the south door there's a large statue of Anson Jones, the president of the Republic of Texas for whom the town is named. Oldtimers sit under shade trees in the courtyard to reminisce and play dominoes. Pigeons make their home high up near the clock.

The Opera House is on the north side of the square, facing the courthouse and challenging it in majesty. It was erected shortly after the turn of the century when that part of the world was booming because of great fields that produced cotton on the surface and oil below. It was used to host theatrical plays created by local people and occasionally by travelling professional troupes that would include famous performers. It is believed that William Jennings Bryan made a speech there in 1914.

The building has three stories, but is at least as tall as the average structure with four floors. The lower level housed a retail business, the top was for storage and the stage was in the middle. When I grew up out there, 40 years after the final real play, my friends and I often sneaked into the old building to have plays of our own, pretending we were Roy Rogers or Gene Autry, arguing about which of them was the greatest cowboy. Duffy Vassar was older and would never let me play a leading role, telling me I was just too young.

Maybe 15 years ago, an eccentric old

bachelor friend of mine bought the Opera House for a ridiculously low price. He lived in it and operated a sort of flea market out of the lower floor, selling used auto parts and all kinds of junk from piles that reached almost to the ceiling.

I once asked him if the building was for sale, dreaming of buying it to restore and make into a dinner theater or museum. He said it wasn't, but that if it ever was, I'd be the first to know. I asked one of the local realtors to keep an eye on it for me.

This summer my friend died and, having no family, left no will. The Opera House became the property of the State of Texas which will soon sell it to the highest bidder. The citizens of Anson have formed a committee and hope to buy it to restore and renovate.

I hope they succeed and host plays there again. Maybe they'll let me come up to play Roy Rogers, the greatest of all the cowboys. If I'm not too old for the part.

A Time to Remember

From Abilene it must be over a hundred miles to the little town of Mercury. For one entire school year when I was in college I preached for the church in Mercury and drove there every Sunday.

It was wonderful.

Mercury sits in lovely oak and cedar country near the Colorado River. From Abilene you go out Highway 36 to Cross Plains. South from there, go past Brownwood Lake and then through the town of Brownwood. Going on south, Mercury is just across the river. Turn left down Main Street. The church building sits up there on the right. That rock building.

There were so many things about that weekly trip I loved. After a typically hard week with the books I'd leave early Sunday morning and drive toward the sunrise. In the fall I watched the trees turn from green to gold and yellow and red. Some Sundays in the winter there was snow in the meadows and on the hillsides. In the spring, fields, carpeted in green, were embroidered with blue and red and pink flowers. There were always deer to count.

The tiny church in Mercury was made up of farmers and ranchers and an elderly widow named Mrs. Cox. They worked out a rotation system where each Sunday I'd eat with a different family and spend the afternoon at their home. I think I'm remembering accurately when I say that not once did they fail to serve me fried chicken. I think it was expected. Then they'd give me a quiet place where I could take a nap or study. I usually did a little of both.

My favorite place to spend the afternoon was at Mrs. Cox's. She made a congealed salad that I thought was the best thing I'd ever tasted. Because I told her so she made it every time. We'd sit at her table, eating that wonderful salad and fried chicken and blackeyed peas, talking about whatever an eighty year old woman and a twenty year old boy could think to talk about. And laughing. She thought I was wonderfully funny.

When we finished eating and visiting I'd help her with the dishes. Then she'd leave me alone until the evening church service. If the weather was pretty I'd walk the mile from her house to the river. Sitting on the bank with my feet in the water I'd think about where it came from and where it was going.

The evening service was at 7 o'clock. That meant I got home way into the dark of night.

Maybe you can understand why it's a nice time to remember.

Sentimental Journey

The greatest adventure of my childhood was when our family made a driving trip to see grandparents in California. It was before the Interstate highway system made travel safer and faster. So we made our way west on old U.S. 180 in a 1949 Ford. I have memories of stopping under trees by the road to eat sandwiches made of Spam and purple onions. And I remember falling in love with that narrow highway.

When I was in West Texas a few weeks ago I took a sentimental journey down a section of that old road. Mollie and I left Anson at 5 o'clock in the morning and drove a hundred and fifty miles to Fort Worth.

Two miles out of town, when there was just the hint of the rising sun in front of us, we passed Mount Hope cemetery where my daddy and all of his family are buried. It sits on a gravelly, windblown hill and is surrounded by a crumbling rock fence. It's home to lots of cotton tails and jackrabbits and horned toads. Individual graves are guarded by twisted, water-starved cedar and mesquite trees. Maybe it will help you to know my daddy if I tell you it's the kind of place where he would have felt right at home.

As we neared Albany we drove by the spot where our school bus almost wrecked in 1959 when I was a high school freshman. We were going to play a football game against the Albany Lions and probably had 60 people on a 48 passenger bus. While we were going down a steep hill the rear tires came off one side and rolled past us and over the side of a cliff. The driver got the bus stopped just before we went over too. Another bus picked us up and took us into town where we got beat 72 to 2.

When we got to Breckenridge I couldn't help but remember Jethro, a dog that belonged to my college roommate and me. On a winter day in the late sixties he was riding with my roommate when the car slid off the icy highway and into a ditch just outside of Breckenridge. The doors flew open and Jethro panicked and ran away.

My friend stayed in town three days while his car was being repaired and spent each day looking for Jethro, but didn't find him. So before he left town he took a description by the police station and asked the officers to please give us a call if they found our dog. A week later they did call with this message: "Boys, we just found your dog outside, scratching on the jailhouse door. We guess he decided to turn himself in."

Tender Memories

Just south of my old hometown, near a curve in a lonely farm to market highway, there's a small wooden cross nailed to the top of a post in a fence that borders a rolling cotton field. It was made by hand almost 15 years ago and placed there to mark the place where one of my friends was killed in a car wreck.

On a Sunday morning in April, while driving out to the small wood-frame country church building where my brother preaches, I saw the cross. The white paint has faded and the red plastic flower that was nailed to it is cracked and brittle, making it obvious it has endured 15 years of harsh West Texas weather.

But it doesn't seem like 15 years since Martha died. Seeing the cross made it as fresh to me as yesterday and brought back the terrible emptiness I felt when I first heard about her wreck. I remembered driving out to the scene and talking softly with friends about how much we hurt, how much we'd lost, and especially how unfair it all seemed.

Martha was two years ahead of me all the way through school. Everybody in my class idolized her because, though she was the most popular girl in her class, she was our friend too. And she was genuinely good. If anybody ever suspected her of doing an immoral thing, I didn't hear about it, and I don't want to hear it now.

When she graduated from high school and married one of her classmates it all seemed just right. In a few years they had a couple of kids and people would say corny things like, "What this country needs is more Rays and Marthas."

But then Ray got sick with cancer and soon died, leaving Martha alone with two small children. They were still small when her car went out of control on that lonely West Texas road.

Someone who loved her built the cross and placed it in the fencerow near where she died as an attempt to state what we all felt then, and I still feel: that sometimes life delivers blows so crushing that only the hope of the Cross makes them bearable.

Places of the Heart

For two weeks I was out of town, enjoying the beauty of Colorado and being with friends I see too seldom. It was a good time away from the things that are familiar, and though no one would mistake me for Willie Nelson, I came back in a laid-back sort of mood.

Mine is a job where that mood is hard to maintain because I'm continually in the presence of the rawest of emotions. I get to share people's joy when babies are born and later when they get married. In the line of duty I attend birthday parties and anniversary celebrations.

But I also get called when people are trying to deal with anguish they're afraid will crush them. Sometimes I find myself in the midst of other people's disputes, trying to keep them from doing things they'll regret. Like the other men in my business, I'm no better or smarter than the next man down the street. And no tougher. So it's hard to stay laid back.

Last week three things happened in one day to remind me that I'm home.

In the morning I went to a nursing home to visit an old gentleman on his birthday. Sitting in a wheelchair, both legs lost in a long term battle with diabetes, he hugged me and said, "Thanks for coming." I visit him often. Sometimes he cries because of his troubles or when he tells me how he misses his wife. But this birthday was a time for smiling and hugging friends to make them feel good.

At noon I was in my pickup approaching a busy intersection where cars were backed up in every direction, none of them moving because a blonde woman, about forty, was walking through the middle of the intersection barefoot, carrying her shoes in one hand and a purse in the other, obviously angry about something. When an elderly woman honked and started to drive through the intersection, the woman yelled and swung the purse at her. Then she squared her shoulders and turned left, marching right down the middle of the only lane going that way, daring somebody to challenge her.

Late in the day I stood in the glaring sun with a very large, tough man who is my good friend, letting him cry and listening to him tell how his daughter died while I was gone. He talked about love and friendship and faith with an eloquence neither of us knew he had. And he told about the ache that hurts him all over. When I told him how my family loves him we stood together and cried.

The day was a good reminder that all the beauty is not in Colorado, and neither are all the mountains.

The Red River Cemetery

In the southern part of Kentucky, just a few miles from where, in 1806, President Andrew Jackson killed Charles Dickinson in a duel arranged in gentlemanly fashion because Dickinson insulted Jackson's wife, there is a very old log church building joined on the east by a cemetery. It's called the Red River Meetinghouse and is a spot of great importance to people who study church history.

I went there last week to try to reconstruct in my mind scenes that occurred more than a hundred and eighty years ago, and to search for the grave of a Presbyterian preacher who died in 1817.

It's not pleasant to report that the building is being allowed to deteriorate and vandals have terribly damaged the cemetery. Granite stones marking graves as old as two hundred years have been pushed over and many broken in half. In the middle of the cemetery are several above-ground graves made of large rectangular stones that are surrounded by a rock fence four feet high and two feet thick. All the graves are from around 1800 and have been broken open. Red dirt fills what's left of them partway up. Parts of the fence have been knocked down.

In a back corner of the cemetery I was able to reconstruct portions of the tragic story of the life of Nathaniel and Ann Munday. I had never heard of them and don't know anybody who has, but somehow the story told by their family plot became important to me.

In 1827 their two year old son, Robert, died. They marked his tiny grave with a piece of coarse granite with his name and the dates of his birth and death chiselled in. He was buried in April when that part of the world is alive with green grass and wildflowers. I closed my eyes and tried to imagine the young father and mother walking away from the cemetery into a beautiful world of color they couldn't possibly have seen.

But life went on for them and I suppose time, to a degree, healed their wound. By 1833 they had five other children. That's how many I have. So I closed my eyes again and tried to imagine the happy sounds of their home. I thought I heard a deep voice laugh and say, "Well, Nat and Annie have another young 'un. We better cut the logs to add 'em another room."

Like you, I love stories with happy endings. But this one doesn't have one. On September 14, 1833 Nathaniel Munday died at age forty-five. Twenty-three days later, in early October, when the air was crisp and the trees aflame with color, three year old Colenia Ann Munday died. Forty-two days after that, in the cold of late November, three month old Nathaniel Junior died. There are two other tiny graves whose markers can no longer be read.

Vandals had knocked over the granite stone that stood at the head of Nathaniel Junior's grave. Mollie and I gently wiped it clean and set it back in place. We did it for Ann Munday, wife and mother.

Books

My daughter Jenny has been assigned a book report. She came to me to discuss the project. I'm glad she did. Daddies need to feel needed about that sort of thing.

We talked about books and reading. I told her that I think reading is about the most exciting thing a person can do. It's a wonderful way of going to places you'll otherwise never go, of doing things you'll otherwise never do, of getting to know people you otherwise never will.

I told her of the things I've experienced while reading. I tried to describe the thrill I had climbing Mount Everest with Sir Edmund Hillary, the terror of sitting in an overcrowded lifeboat and watching the Titanic sink beneath icy waters, and the loss of emotion as time wore on at Auschwitz.

More than 20 years ago I read Louis Cochran's "The Fool of God." It was a startlingly emotional experience that I hadn't expected. When Alexander's first child died I actually felt grief. When a second child contracted the same sickness and also died my own grief intensified. When Margaret, the wife and mother, got sick I found myself praying for her recovery. At her death, as Alexander fell sobbing beside her bed, I cried too.

That night I walked outside and stared into a star-filled sky. I had seen it with friends many times before. But realizing it was the same sky Alexander and Margaret and their children had seen and loved gave it a new meaning. Cochran's historical novel had made one of history's great men into a person I felt I knew as a friend.

More than 30 years ago I read of Ralph Edward's escape from the city to live on a lake in British Columbia. He lived there alone. Yet through the miracle of reading I and a million others lived there too. We cut every log with him as he hurried to build a cabin before the onslaught of winter. We caught lake trout and fried them for breakfast. We fought off grizzly bears. We listened to howling wolves on still nights.

I told my Jenny that she too can do all those things and more. All she has to do is learn to love reading. What excites me is that I think she understood. In fact, she's off right now with a boy named Billy and two dogs named Old Dan and Little Ann. They're hunting raccoons where the red fern grows.

Leaving Home

My young friend Margaret is a freshman at Texas Tech, away from home for the first time, unsure whether she's a girl or a woman. Because she's important to me, and because I know what it can be like to leave home, I wrote her what I hope will be an encouraging letter.

Back in the fifties, in hard times, one of my older brothers quit school to join the Navy. It wasn't what he wanted, but circumstances made it necessary. So, at 17, he became a sailor.

He was told to report to a naval station in California by midnight on a certain date. Daddy and Mother decided that somehow we'd take him there rather than send him by bus. So we drove to the west coast, some of the time sad because we were going to leave Johnny, and other times excited about the adventure.

We spent his last day as a civilian playing in the Pacific, trying to keep things lighthearted by making silly West Texas jokes about the ocean. "It's not as big as I thought it'd be." "It reminds me of that dove-huntin' tank on Joe Steele's place."

When the day was over, at midnight, we drove through a gate and past a military policeman, onto U.S. Navy property. The whole place was paved with asphalt, without a tree or blade of grass anywhere. Rows of three-story white barracks were bathed in yellow light.

My 17 year old big brother went into a small building to report in, coming back in a few minutes to tell us bye. "Bye, Mama. Bye, Daddy." "Bye, Son." "Bye, Kids." "Bye, Johnny." Then he blinked his eyes and ducked his head as he walked toward a barracks building, looking back only once to wave. We waved back and then drove through the yellow light and past the M.P. and his gate, feeling emptier than we thought we could stand.

In time Johnny was on the USS Kear-

29

sarge, out in the Caribbean and later near Japan, having the time of his life. His letters told strange stories about flying fish, weird characters, beautiful sunsets and jet airplanes taking off and landing on his ship. He told our mother to get ready because when he got home he'd have a music box and cuckoo clock for her.

I needed to tell my young friend Margaret that as tough as it can be to leave home, there really does come a time you've got to do it. And, if you travel carefully, the road from home leads to lots of really good things.

So hang in there, Kid.

I may need to tell her mother, too.

Watching and Waiting

It's just before dark on this Saturday in late August. I'm sitting in my front yard, watching a storm move in from the north while I wait for my family to drive in from Mississippi. Not wanting them on the road after dark, and for sure not in a Texas thunderstorm, I'm hoping they get here soon.

The storm looks like a good one. There's already a strong, wet-feeling wind blowing in my face, with the rain still miles away. I can see plenty of lightning and the sound of its thunder is getting louder. A little boy from down the street just rode by on his bicycle and shouted over the wind, "It feels pretty good, don't it Mr. Middlebrook?" I yelled back, "Yes, get home!"

The coolness does feel good after a day of 95 degree heat and high humidity that have driven me to my second bath since noon. I took the first one after working outside all morning, thinking it would get the job done 'til tomorrow. But about 4 o'clock I spent just a little more time doing some light outside work and got really sweaty again. So I bathed again, and I guess you could say I'm out here getting a blow dry. Fully clothed.

The storm's a lot closer now and the wind's getting stronger, shaking and twisting the trees across the street. I've had to move to my porch because a stinging rain has started falling. Lightning is slamming the ground closer and closer, its thunder now exploding angrily around me. Fear is trying to drive me inside, away from the lightning, but is having a tough battle with fascination, which is keeping me right here.

The neighbor boy just pedaled by again, his head ducked as he pushed against the wind and the driving rain. I shouted, "I said get home!" He twisted his tucked-in head and said, "OK."

It's dark now and the storm's not showing any signs of letting up. My family's still out there somewhere.

Fall

I was raised in hot country, a part of the world where summer can be amazingly harsh. I have memories of entire summers of searing heat and a total absence of rain when cracks would open in the ground and gradually widen as the sun poured down day after day. Discouraged farmers with tears rolling down the dirt on their faces would plow up cotton crops that never grew. The sky would darken from the dust that at times literally blotted out the sun.

In those drought years we looked forward to the end of summer. As early as the middle of August people started commenting about being able to feel fall in the air. It wasn't that it was cool, but just that there was something about the way the sky looked and the air felt that made you know a change was coming. Or maybe it was wishful thinking.

By the middle of October the change would be dramatic, with the early cool fronts bringing the possibility of slow, thunderless rains that would last two or three days.

I remember what I thought was a great joke my daddy made one year when we had such a rain very early, probably in September. The temperature dropped to about 70 degrees. I was standing close to Daddy when he asked some of his friends, "Think it'll snow?" Everybody laughed. The truth was that the weather had them feeling so good that every joke was a great one.

When the wonderful north wind blew the clouds away the sky would actually sparkle it was so cool and clear. You wanted to throw your head back and breathe as deep as you could.

Our favorite of all things was done in the fall.

Dove season opened the first day of September. We loaded our own shotgun shells and hunted every day until the sun set. Early afternoons were spent walking through recently harvested grain fields flushing birds while they were feeding. Later we would sit next to stock tanks shooting the birds as they came for water. We thought, and I still think the Lord provided them for us to hunt and eat.

When we'd get home Mother would fry the doves and prepare biscuits and gravy and okra and potatoes to go with them. When we were lucky she'd make a peach cobbler.

It's the middle of August now. Early one morning go outside and see if you don't feel a touch of fall in the air. See if it doesn't excite you.

The Old House

After my brothers and sisters built our mother a new house, we tore down her old one, using hammers and crowbars and a borrowed tractor. Without trying to save anything, we ripped it apart, hauling the debris away to a landfill south of town.

In some ways it was fun and felt good. Ma was moving into a new brick house, well-insulated against the heat and cold of West Texas, centrally air-conditioned. That after more than 40 years in an uninsulated, two bedroom house in which she and Daddy raised 12 kids. Who would have trouble understanding the excitement we felt about seeing her in a new house with the thickest carpet in town?

When the job was completed there was nothing left but a bare spot on the ground. From the road you could see our mother standing, beaming from the porch of the new house on the back of the property. "Smile Ma, and let us take your picture."

But there are other ways in which that exciting day was full of sadness. That old house held memories of an entire family's history. No matter how much we told ourselves the memories were really in our hearts, the thought of tearing it down made us feel empty. Most of us took a last, private trip through the house, touching walls and floors, trying to hear again the laughter that had always lived there, hurting again when we remembered the tears that had sometimes visited.

When Ma had gone through the house the last time we took a heavy chain and snaked it through the house and out a door on one end and a window on the other. Then we tied the chain together and attached it to the tractor. When we had everyone out of the way, my oldest brother shouted, "Go!" The tractor moved, breaking wood and glass, leaving a dozen grown people standing, looking, unsure whether to smile or cry.

Mixed Emotions

My son Samuel and I are sitting together in my bedroom, quietly reading and listening to soft music, talking only occasionally, and I'm thinking about the day we tore Ma's house down.

I looked over at Sam a moment ago, amazed at his size and that he's in the third grade. He's the youngest of five and undeniable evidence that time is continuing its work, changing everything it touches and touching everything.

The late afternoon sunlight is filtering through the west window to my back, creating designs on the foot of my bed and the closet door across the room. There's a coolness coming through the open window, convincing evidence that, in late September, the seasons are also changing.

Mollie and I moved into this house fifteen years ago, excited because it was a nice house and we were coming to a good job. But after fifteen years, shared with each other and the kids, it's more than a house. It's home.

Lately we've talked about moving to another house, better suited to a family the size of ours, on a few acres, with a pond and trees.

But today, as the last rays of the day's sunlight fade from my closet door what earlier seemed like such a good idea has some question marks. I've been thinking about a time, years ago, when we traded cars. We were all excited when we drove our old car to pick up the new one. But when it came time to exchange keys with the salesman our three year old daughter was crying, upset because we were leaving the old car.

Sometimes forty year old men are a lot like three year old girls.

41

West Texas Football

More than two decades ago I played on a high school football team that won only one game in two seasons. In West Texas that is considered a serious failure that brings shame to an entire community. The citizens of our little town had to live with the embarrassment of our record while knowing that 30 miles to the east, in Albany, old-timers sat on the town-square playing dominoes beneath a gigantic football shaped sign that read, "State Champions."

We lost once by a score of 72 to 2. At halftime the score was 72 to 0. In the second half the other team kept punting to us on first down. Finally their quarterback took a snap from center and receded back into his own end zone. We chased around after him, not able to catch him. After a while he dramatically fell down. A giggling referee clasped his hands together over his head, signaling a safety.

Jeannie C. Riley was one of our cheerleaders. She and the rest of them cheered their hearts out. But none of it helped. Her shame was so great that she moved away to Nashville to sing country music. Several of us ballplayers went into preaching. Our coach disappeared and was never heard from again. The belief was that he had moved to New York. Some of the local philosophers said it was the only thing they could think of that he could do.

The one game we did win was against the Hamlin Pied Pipers. It was a glorious victory on a cold and wet Friday night that set off a weekend of community-wide celebration. The highlight of the revelry occurred on Saturday morning when one of the local businessmen invited the whole football team down to the local drug store where he bought us all cherry phosphates. It was wonderful!

But sometimes at night I wake up in a cold sweat thinking what it must have been like in Hamlin on that Saturday morning. The Pied Piper players had to answer that awful question, "You got beat by WHOM?"

The Quiet Fan

Almost every night for the past two weeks my family has driven down FM 1960, through Humble and across Lake Houston, to watch one of Tomball's all-star baseball teams play in a tournament at Huffman. The baseball's been only a part of the fun.

In the first game one of our players was trying to score and ran over the other team's catcher, leaving him sprawling on the ground. The umpire said to our player, loud enough for everybody on the east side of Lake Houston to hear, "Son, you gotta slide when there's a play at home. Do that again and you're outta the game." But then the fans on the other side started yelling, "He can't do that. He's gotta go." So the umpire said, even louder than before, "That's it, son. Ya gotta go," and threw him out of the game.

Some of our fans make a lot of noise, shouting encouragement to our players, yelling at the bad guys and groaning at the umpire's calls. But not me. I sit quietly and watch what's happening and never say a word. Never! But in one game the other team kept griping about everything. Finally, when one of their batters frowned in open disgust at the umpire's call and then glared at our pitcher, I said softly and respectfully, "Come on Parkwood. Quit your whinin' and play baseball." The batter threw his bat down and told me to shut up. Then when he walked, he yelled at me again on his way to first base. The umpire stopped the game for a few minutes and told everyone to calm down.

By taking them out to supper and promising I wouldn't embarrass them again, I talked my family into going back the next night. But it might have been a mistake in that I was made the object of a cruel joke.

I'm not going to tell who the jokesters were because Joe Fuqua and Philip Pasafuma both have good reputations in this town that I don't want to hurt. But here's what they did.

I was sitting in my lawn chair up next to the dugout by first base, quietly watching the ballgame and drinking a big orange drink, maintaining the family's dignity. The bleachers behind me were full of Tomball people, including the two unnamed parties mentioned above.

Like any person raised in West Texas would have done, I had taken my shoes off and was resting my feet on them. At one point I picked up one foot and in a manly way rested it on the other knee, still drinking my big orange drink and watching the game. The two unnamed friends sneaked up and took away my shoe in full view of all the Tomball people behind me.

To hear them tell it later, the best moment of all was when I put my foot down and, without looking, patted around in search of my shoe for about five minutes while I finished my big orange drink and watched the game. When I finally turned around and realized what was happening, the two unnamed men were holding their sides and shaking. So were the other people in the bleachers.

If you find out who the two unnamed men were, don't hold it against them. They're really good guys who just got carried away.

Our team's doing good. I hope they keep winning so they can go to another tournament. For some reason my wife said she hopes they don't.

A Texas Patriot

When I was in college a couple of decades ago I was exposed for the first time to people from states other than Texas, people who actually thought there were ways in which their states were better than Texas. Something most people don't know is that the reason I'm weak in math and the sciences is that I sacrificed time less loyal Texans used for study to defend the state's honor against enemies that had secretly stolen into Abilene, the very heart of the state.

What made an adequate defense so difficult was that many of them could look almost exactly like Texans, wearing jeans and boots and plaid shirts. Some of them even had letter jackets or sweaters with A's or C's or S's on the front.

And they would behave in the most normal ways most of the time, talking about sports or politics or the war in Viet Nam. But then, often out of the blue, one would say something like, "I can't wait to leave this place and get back to God's country." I, of course, thought they were talking about getting away from college and back to Amarillo or Waxahachie. I can't describe how shocked I was to learn they were talking about getting away from Texas and back to Colorado, or even California. I'm not easy to hurt but that hurt.

Even worse was the fact that many of my fellow Texans spent a great amount of time fraternizing with those people, and some actually sided with them openly. They'd say things like, "I know what you mean. I've lived here all my life and when I get the chance I'm moving to Denver."

I fought back with able arguments about the fact that Texas was the biggest and most beautiful of all the states and that it had the smartest and most talented people. When some Coloradan would say, "That just don't add up," I'd tell him to keep addition out of it, that I was weak in math and the sciences.

My best arguments were about Texas sunrises and sunsets. I'd study them carefully to be able to describe them in detail when some Coloradan would try to tell me there was nothing in Texas to compare to watching an eagle fly high over a stand of yellow aspen on the western slope in October, while listening to the singing of a mountain stream.

On this Tuesday morning at the end of July I'm sitting alone by a campfire, facing Mt. Elbert in Colorado, watching the sunrise. What makes it curious is that I'm facing west, away from the sun, waiting for the first rays to hit the tip of the mountain. When it happens the light then comes racing down the mountain until it envelopes you.

Right now there's a stringy cloud over the mountain's peak and the sunlight hitting it has colored it orange and purple. I looked around a moment ago and the whole sky over the mountains behind me is the same color.

Last night late I sat in this same spot to watch the mountain. An almost full moon was hidden from my view by the clouds, its light reaching only the snow-covered peak. Coyotes were calling and answering each other in the valley below.

Yesterday I sat in shirt sleeves and watched a storm across on the mountain that left it covered in fresh snow. When it ended the sky behind the white peak was a deep, clear blue.

I really still feel the same about Texas as I did 25 years ago. But I am beginning to think I might should have spent a little more energy studying math and science.

Barefoot In The Snow

A man shouldn't go outside barefoot when it's twenty-five degrees and snowing. Besides the physical danger it sets up an embarrassing situation for his wife and children. If word gets out they have to deal with hard questions from friends and schoolmates. It's not a pleasant thing for a woman to be in a beauty salon and have someone shout to her above the noise of the hairdryers, "Hey, why was your husband out in the snow barefoot last night?" And it's not easy for a kid at school to answer that question about her daddy. People think they might know why.

So you can understand why I hesitate to mention that on January 31 I did spend a few minutes outside in the snow with my shoes off. But there is a very good reason. To relieve the social pressure on my family I'll explain.

One year ago some of our friends had the water pipes in their attic freeze and burst. The amount of damage done was amazing. And I inspected every bit of it. I saw the carpet ripped out of an entire house, mattresses laid outside to dry on sawhorses, and sheetrock and insulation laying wet and ugly on dressers and tables. I watched our friends endure weeks of frustration and inconvenience as they got their house back in shape.

Having been taught by my daddy to study life and learn from it I decided I'd try hard to never let the pipes in my house freeze.

Which brings us to January 31. The temperature in the morning was about forty degrees. Cold and uncomfortable, but not freezing. The forecast called for it to drop to near twenty that night. By my calculations that meant that I should go out and drip my faucets around 10 o'clock. I figured the temperature would not drop below twenty-eight degrees before then. (My daddy taught me how to figure those kinds of things). Past history had taught me that our faucets don't freeze until it's twenty-seven degrees.

At sundown I was sitting in my easy chair with my shoes off, reading a magazine. One of the kids came up and asked if I knew it was twenty-five degrees and snowing outside. Very calmly I knocked the chair over and burst out the front door. When I got to the front faucet and turned it on nothing happened.

I shouted for one of my kids to plug in an extension cord and stretch it out to me. I told another one to bring a hairdryer quick. For the next several minutes I alternately blew the hot air on my feet to keep them warm and the faucet to thaw it. It worked. Soon there was the wonderful sound of running water. I left it dripping and went back to my easy chair to read.

That's the whole story. I hope now for the sake of my family people will stop talking about their husband and daddy.

I Love You Mollie, But . .

There was a time, more than a few years ago, that I possessed some pretty imposing credentials as a bachelor. When I got engaged at age 25, a college editor included this statement in his paper: "The shock caused by the announcement was intensified by the fact that Middlebrook has long been considered a staunch advocate of non-marital bachelorism and a bastion of strength to the cause of unitary celibacy." What he meant was he thought I'd never get married.

This week my wife is in Mississippi and I'm learning that whatever talent I may have had for being a bachelor has eroded with time. I haven't been alone even a day and here I am, past 11 o'clock at night, with an unmade bed, dirty clothes on the bathroom floor, a sink full of dirty dishes and not much food in the house for breakfast.

Since my vacuum cleaner was making funny noises, I've got it laying in about 10 pieces on the dirty carpet.

I've studied the dirty clothes situation and have decided to try to deal with it, using my wife's washing machine. It opens from the top and inside has a sort of teepee-like cylinder with ridges where it fans out at the bottom. My bet is that the cylinder turns and stirs the water like the propeller on a bass boat. There's a dial on the front with four or five settings, none of which mean anything definite to me. I'll pick one and work under the theory that any washing at all will beat the current situation.

One thing I'm convinced of is that washing dishes is like riding a bicycle. Once you've learned to do it you never forget. When I was in high school I worked in the cafeteria as a dishwasher and, if I say it myself, developed a very efficient system of holding the dishes in my left hand to swab them with the right before laying them on the counter to dry. I don't see any reason why the system won't work here, though it would be nice if Chester Calhoun was here to mop the floor when I'm done like he was in the school cafeteria.

Before Mollie left, she bought what she said was enough groceries to last the whole time she's gone. But, strange enough for a woman who cooks as good as she does, what she bought seems nearly useless. My pantry is full of rice, flour, potatoes and all sorts of canned vegetables and the freezer's got raw meats in it. I do have enough peanut butter for breakfast and can go tomorrow to buy ice cream and sardines and ready-made burritos.

I've got a friend who told me once, when his wife was out of town, that as much as he loves her, if he lost her on Monday, he'd have another wife by the weekend. He said he wasn't talking about romance but survival. Here at midnight, hungry, with vacuum cleaner parts spread across the floor, I understand him.

Life's Seasons Pass Quickly

Just the other day my first baby was born. Or anyway, it seems like just the other day.

I was talking to my mother-in-law and busily counting the angels on the pink and blue wallpaper of Methodist Hospital's "stork club" when a smiling nurse named Pearlie announced that I was the father of a beautiful baby girl.

I wish I could describe the feeling that announcement gave me. It was a mixture of a sort of love I'd never known, pride, and fear of the new responsibility. The feeling has never left me for even a minute.

It didn't take me long to learn the most wonderful lessons. Things like how a baby looks and smells all freshly bathed and dressed for bed in a gown with pictures of rocking horses on it and a draw string at the bottom. Things like how good a backache can feel when it comes from sitting too long in one position so your baby can sleep against your chest. Things like how a baby will smile when you gently blow in its face.

I have five children now. My littlest is eight years old and in the third grade. But it doesn't seem possible. The time has been too short for that.

Now, instead of mixing formula and changing diapers, Mollie and I go to ballgames and sign report cards. We're learning to adjust to the kids' broadening world and their lessening dependence on us. And we wonder aloud how the clock can be slowed before this time too is gone.

On a recent Sunday morning I stopped at a convenience store while on the way to church. There was a mother with a very small baby checking out in front of me. When she was gone the cashier said to me, "I'll bet you can remember when you had babies that small."

That startled me. Is it obvious even to a stranger that that season of my life is gone? Did she know what wonderful memories I do have? Did she know that as much as I am enjoying the present I miss having a baby sleep on my chest?

Maybe some of you younger parents will lend me your babies for a day or two. But don't lend them out too long. Take advantage of every day. Believe me when I tell you that life's seasons pass quickly.